Collins

Easy Learning

Mental maths practice

Age 7-9

My name is _____.

I am _____ years old.

I go to _____ School.

My birthday is _____.

Peter Clarke

How to use this book

- Find a quiet, comfortable place to work, away from other distractions.
- Ask your child what maths topic they are doing at school, and choose an appropriate topic.
- Tackle one topic at a time.
- Help with reading the instructions where necessary, and ensure that your child understands what they are required to do.
- Help and encourage your child to check their own answers as they complete each activity.
- Discuss with your child what they have learnt.
- Let your child return to their favourite pages once they have been completed, to play the games and talk about the activities.
- Reward your child with plenty of praise and encouragement.

Special features

- Yellow boxes: Introduce and outline the key maths ideas.
- Example boxes: Show how to do the activity.
- Yellow shaded boxes: Offer advice to parents on how to consolidate your child's understanding.
- Games: Some of the topics include a game, which reinforces the topic. Some of these games require a spinner. This is easily made using a pencil, a paperclip and the circle printed on each games page. Gently flick the paperclip with your finger to make it spin.

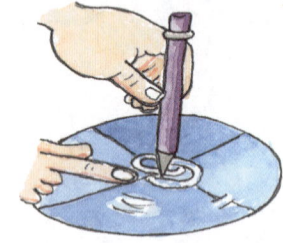

Published by Collins
An imprint of HarperCollins*Publishers*
77–85 Fulham Palace Road
Hammersmith
London
W6 8JB

Browse the complete Collins catalogue at
www.collinseducation.com

© HarperCollins*Publishers* Limited 2013

10 9 8 7 6 5 4 3 2

ISBN-13 978-0-00-750505-0

The author asserts his moral right to be identified as the author of this work.

The author wishes to thank Brian Molyneaux for his valuable contribution to this publication.

All rights reserved. No part of this publication may be reproduced, stored in a retrieval system, or transmitted in any form or by any means, electronic, mechanical, photocopying, recording or otherwise, without the prior written permission of the Publisher or a licence permitting restricted copying in the United Kingdom issued by the Copyright Licensing Agency Ltd., 90 Tottenham Court Road, London W1T 4LP.

British Library Cataloguing in Publication Data

A Catalogue record for this publication is available from the British Library

Written by Peter Clarke
Page design by G Brasnett, Cambridge
Illustrated by Kathy Baxendale, Rachel Annie Bridgen and Graham Smith
Cover design by Linda Miles, Lodestone Publishing Ltd
Cover illustration by Kathy Baxendale
Commissioned by Tammy Poggo
Project managed by Chantal Peacock
Production by Rebecca Evans
Printed in China

MIX
Paper from
responsible sources
FSC™ C007454

FSC™ is a non-profit international organisation established to promote the responsible management of the world's forests. Products carrying the FSC label are independently certified to assure consumers that they come from forests that are managed to meet the social, economic and ecological needs of present and future generations, and other controlled sources.

Find out more about HarperCollins and the environment at
www.harpercollins.co.uk/green

Contents

How to use this book	2
Numbers 1	4
Addition and subtraction 1	6
Multiplication and division 1	8
Fractions and decimals 1	10
Shape, space and measures 1	12
Problems and puzzles 1	14
Quick Check 1	16
Time Test 1	17
Numbers 2	18
Addition and subtraction 2	20
Multiplication and division 2	22
Fractions and decimals 2	24
Shape, space and measures 2	26
Problems and puzzles 2	28
Quick Check 2	30
Time Test 2	31
Answers	32

Numbers 1

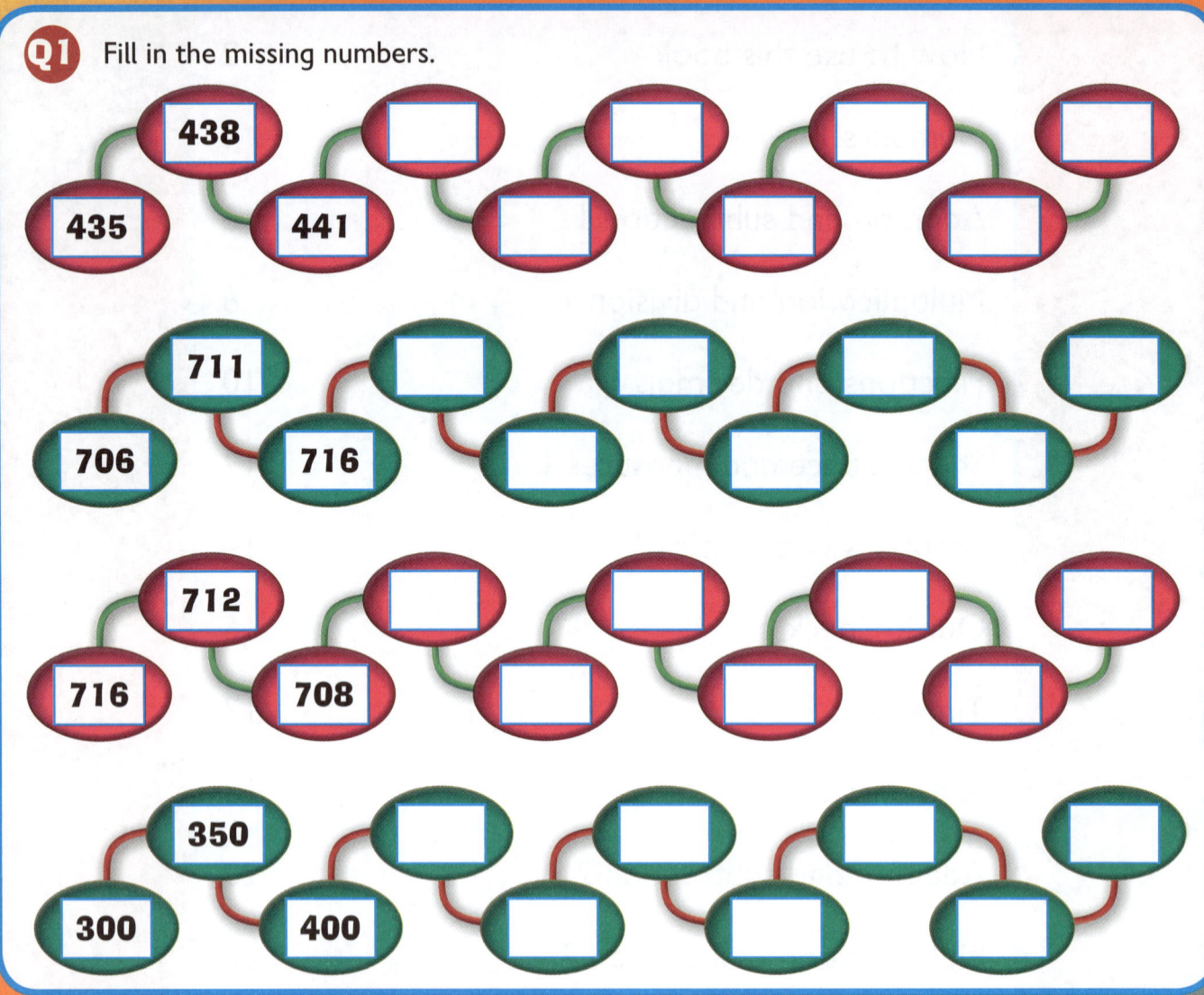

Q1 Fill in the missing numbers.

[Number chains:
- 435, 438, 441, ...
- 706, 711, 716, ...
- 716, 712, 708, ...
- 300, 350, 400, ...]

Q2 Use the < or > sign to complete these statements.

| 695 ___ 703 | 544 ___ 424 | 756 ___ 675 |
| 119 ___ 209 | 843 ___ 834 | 297 ___ 379 |

Look at all the numbers in the blue boxes.
Write these numbers in order, smallest first.

☐ ☐ ☐ ☐ ☐ ☐

Look at all the numbers in the red boxes.
Write these numbers in order, smallest first.

☐ ☐ ☐ ☐ ☐ ☐

Game: Larger number wins

You need: pack of playing cards with the Jacks, Queens and Kings removed, counters
- Shuffle the cards and place them face down in a pile.
- Take turns to:
  - pick the top three cards
  - arrange the cards to make a three-digit number and read it out, i.e.
  - place one of your counters on a box on the grid that fits that description.

- If you can't find that answer on the grid, miss that turn.
- After each player has had a turn, collect up all the cards and shuffle them again.
- The winner is the first player to complete a line of 4 counters. A line can go horizontally or vertically.

>700	less than 850	>100	>200	<400
less than 800	<650	>400	>300	more than 600
less than 750	<200	more than 250	more than 650	less than 350
<600	>550	less than 700	>800	<250
less than 450	more than 500	<300	<500	more than 800

Q3 Complete each number sentence.

697 = 600 + ☐ + 7   423 = 400 + 20 + ☐

391 = ☐ + 90 + 1   725 = ☐ + 20 + 5

284 = 200 + ☐ + 4   139 = 100 + ☐ + ☐

572 = ☐ + ☐ + 2   918 = 900 + ☐ + ☐

In order to calculate with numbers, it is important that your child is able to count, recognise, read, write, compare, order and round numbers to 1000 then 10 000. They also need to have a secure understanding of place value, i.e. 582 = 500 + 80 + 2.

Addition and subtraction 1

Q1 Answer these.

9 + 4 = ☐   6 + 11 = ☐   17 − 8 = ☐

7 + 7 = ☐   13 − 6 = ☐   14 + 6 = ☐

15 − 8 = ☐   13 + 5 = ☐   16 − 3 = ☐

18 − 12 = ☐   19 − 10 = ☐   12 + 7 = ☐

8 − 5 = ☐   7 + 4 + 5 = ☐ 17 − 4 = ☐

6 + 14 = ☐   12 + 7 = ☐   3 + 8 + 6 = ☐

20 − 12 = ☐   14 − 9 = ☐   15 + 3 = ☐

6 + 8 + 9 = ☐ 8 + 8 = ☐   16 − 14 = ☐

Q2 Complete the diagrams.

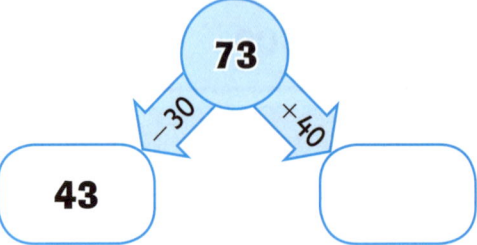

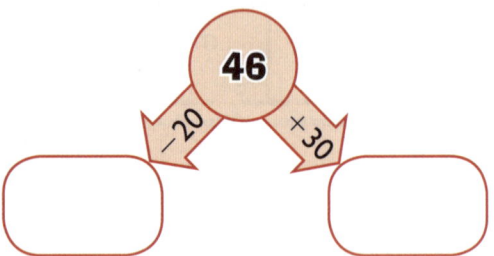

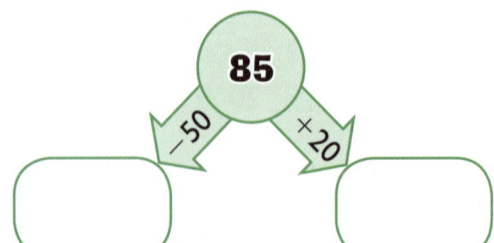

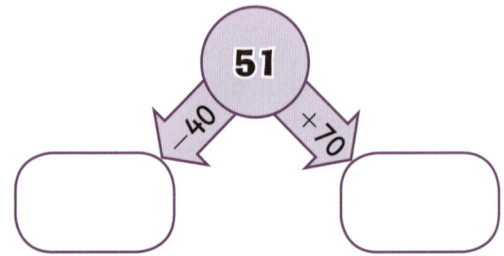

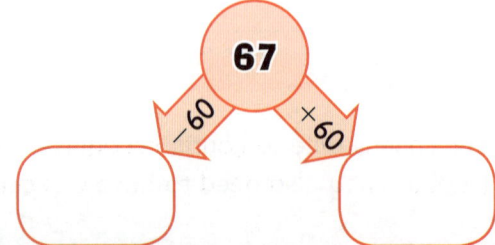

Game: Difference of the totals

You need: paperclip, pencil and paper

- Take turns to spin both spinners and add the two numbers together.
- The player with the larger total wins that round.
- Their score is the difference between the two totals.
- Keep a running total.
- The winner is the first player to score 30 points or more.

Q3 Complete the diagrams.

Being able to confidently add and subtract a one-digit number and a multiple of 10 to or from a two-digit number will help your child when adding and subtracting pairs of two-digit numbers such as 68 + 47 and 73 − 25.

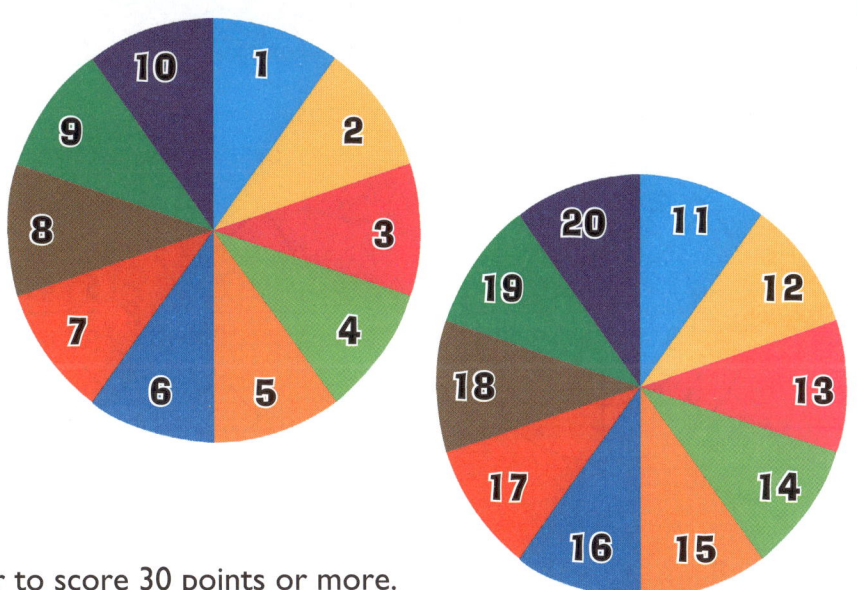

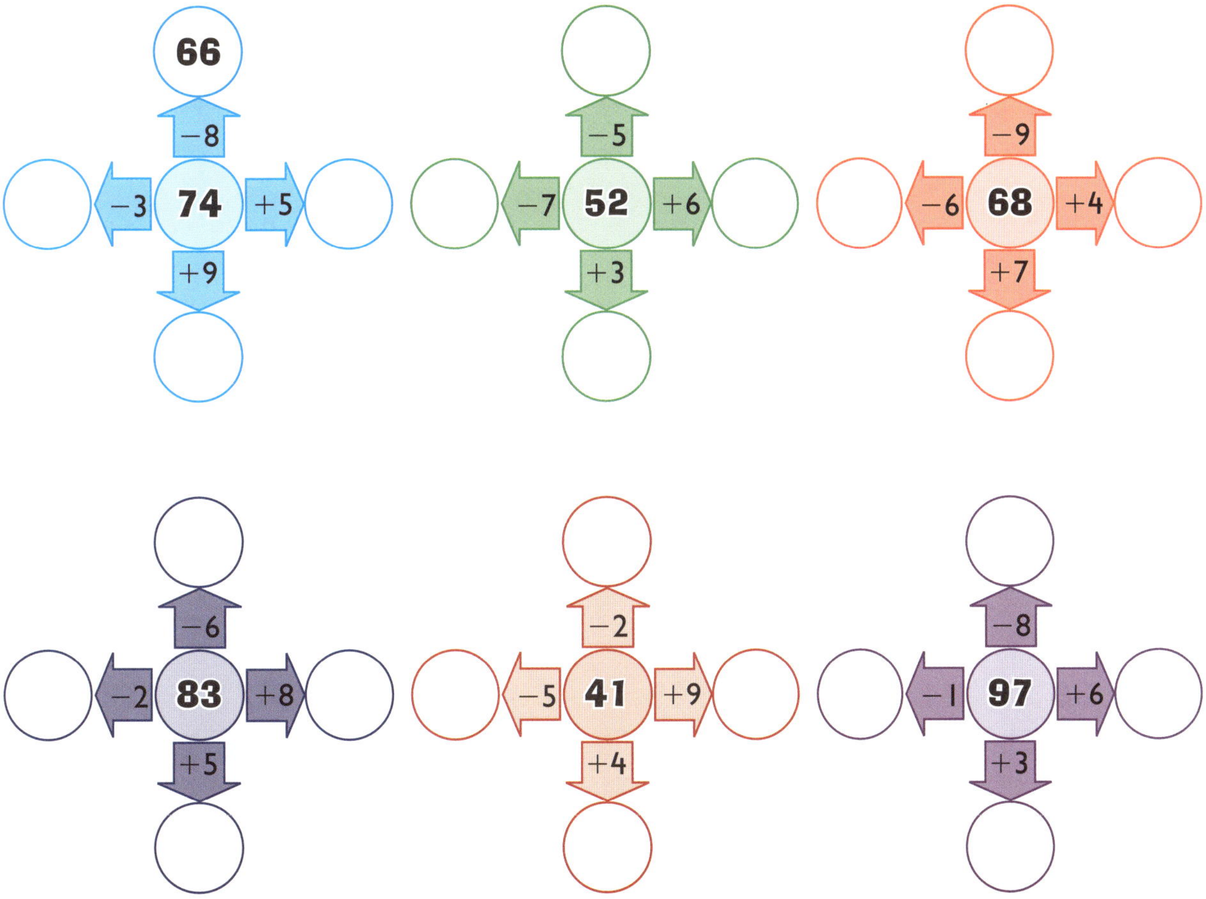

Multiplication and division 1

Q1 Complete the multiplication rings.

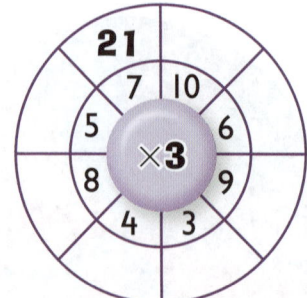  

 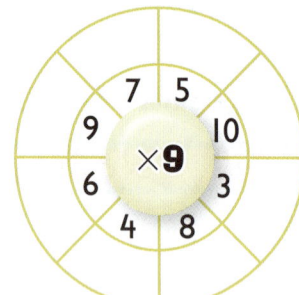 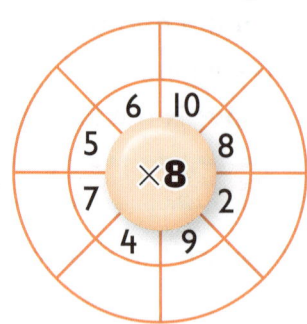

Q2 Complete each bubble puzzle.

÷6: 42→7, 36→☐, 54→☐, 30→☐, 12→☐, 60→☐, 24→☐, 48→☐, 18→☐

÷8: 24→☐, 80→☐, 48→☐, 16→☐, 72→☐, 64→☐, 40→☐, 56→☐, 32→☐

÷4: 20→☐, 8→☐, 36→☐, 28→☐, 40→☐, 16→☐, 24→☐, 32→☐, 12→☐

÷9: 36→☐, 18→☐, 81→☐, 45→☐, 63→☐, 90→☐, 27→☐, 72→☐, 54→☐

÷3: 12→☐, 27→☐, 18→☐, 24→☐, 6→☐, 15→☐, 21→☐, 9→☐, 30→☐

÷7: 63→☐, 70→☐, 14→☐, 28→☐, 56→☐, 49→☐, 35→☐, 42→☐, 21→☐

Game: Quick tables

You need: 2 paper clips, 2 pencils, 20 counters

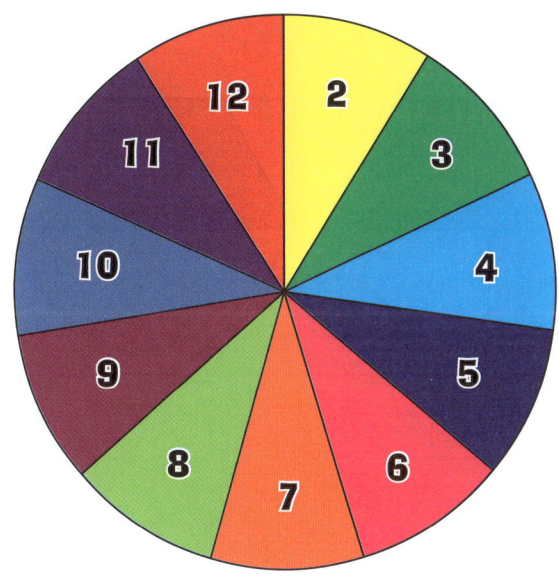 

- Each player spins a spinner.
- Both players multiply the two numbers together.
- The first player to call out the correct answer wins that round and takes a counter.
- The overall winner is the first player to collect 10 counters.

Q3 Complete each tower.

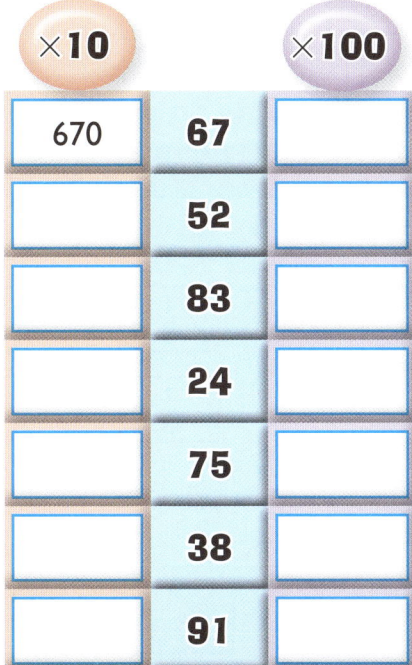

×10	×100		÷10	÷100
670	67		30	300
	52			8700
	83			5200
	24			6000
	75			1800
	38			2900
	91			400

Being able to recall the answers to the times tables facts up to 10 × 10, and the related division facts, will help your child when multiplying and dividing larger numbers such as 34 × 6 and 83 ÷ 4.

Fractions and decimals 1

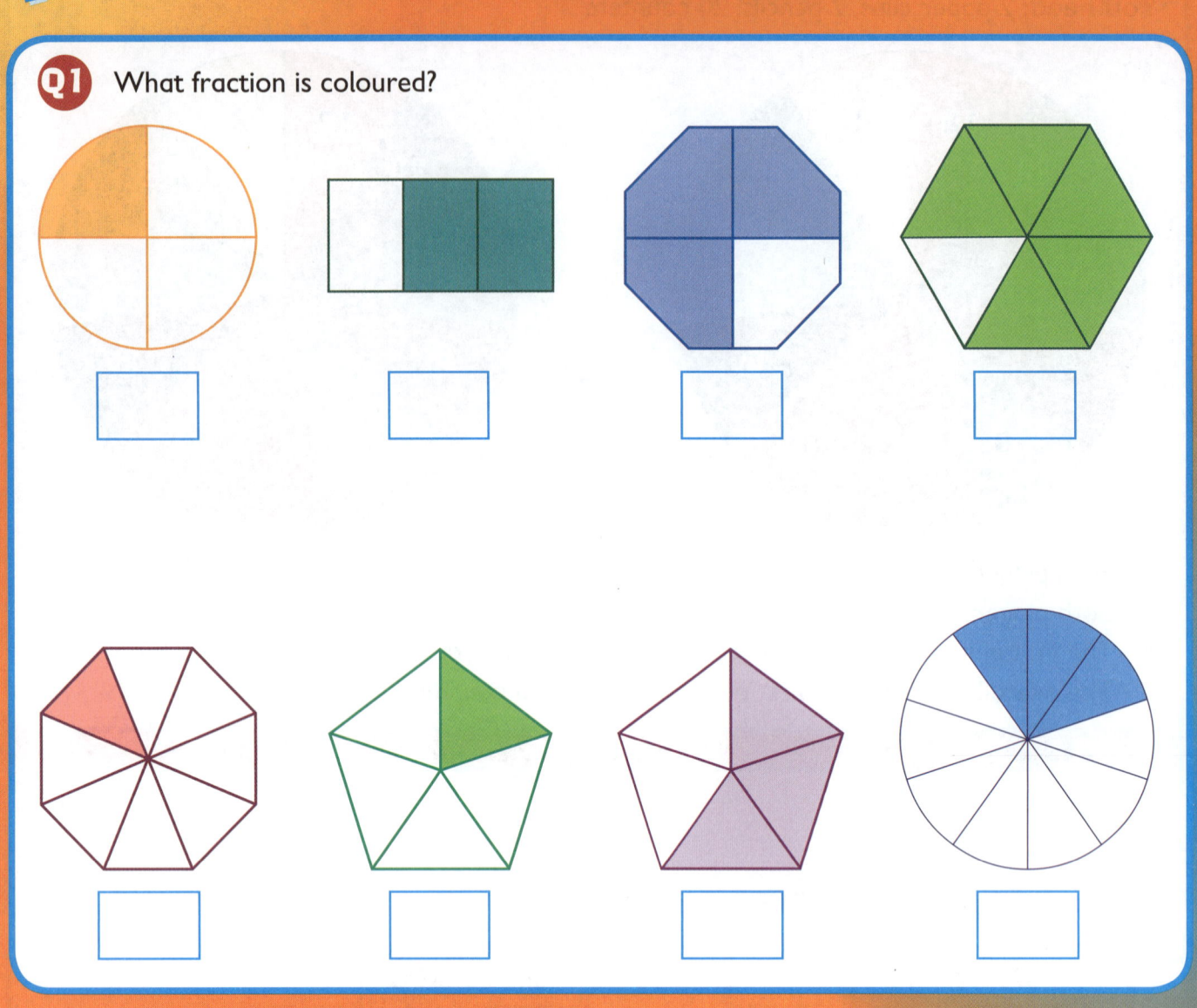

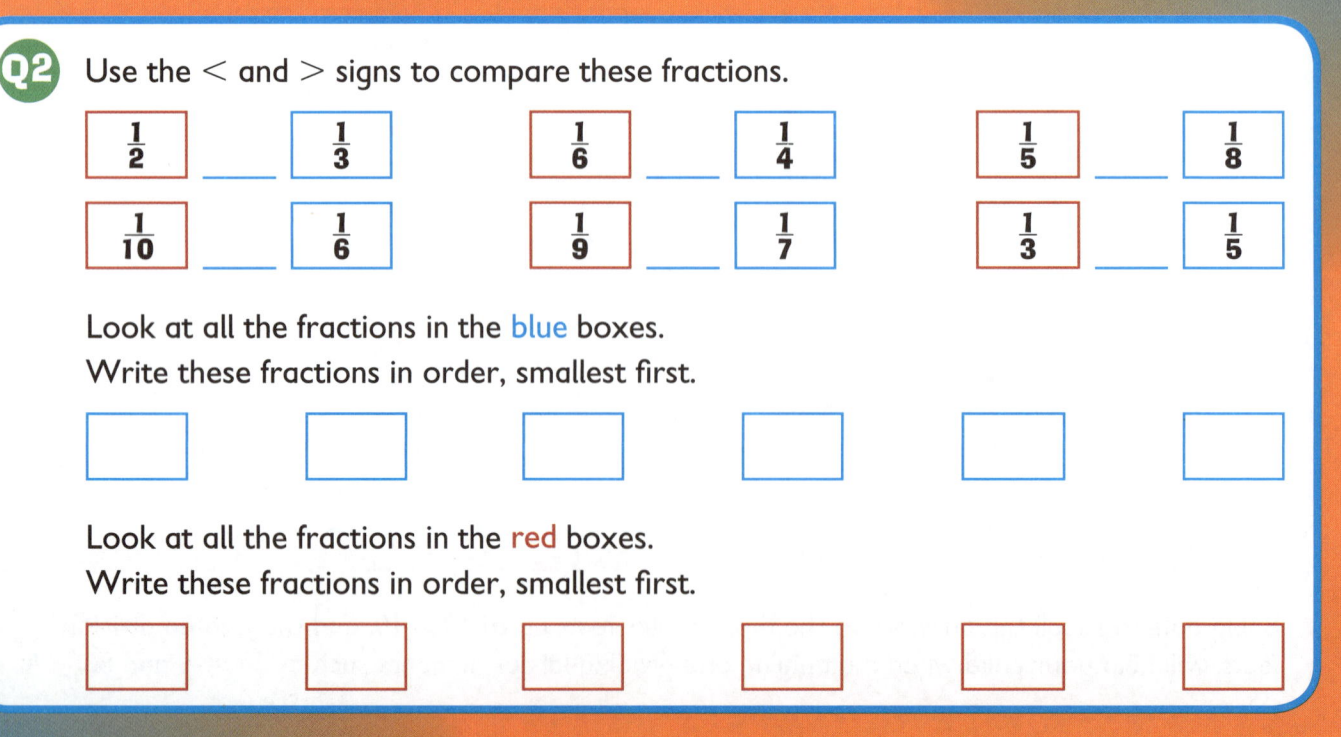

Q1 What fraction is coloured?

[shapes with fractions coloured, each with an empty box below]

Q2 Use the < and > signs to compare these fractions.

| 1/2 __ 1/3 | 1/6 __ 1/4 | 1/5 __ 1/8 |
| 1/10 __ 1/6 | 1/9 __ 1/7 | 1/3 __ 1/5 |

Look at all the fractions in the blue boxes.
Write these fractions in order, smallest first.

[ ] [ ] [ ] [ ] [ ] [ ]

Look at all the fractions in the red boxes.
Write these fractions in order, smallest first.

[ ] [ ] [ ] [ ] [ ] [ ]

Game: Halves and quarters

You need: pencil, paperclip, counters

- Take turns to:
  - spin both spinners
  - multiply the number by the fraction
  - put a counter on the answer on the grid.
- If you can't find the answer on the grid, miss that turn.
- The winner is the first player to complete a line of 3 counters. A line can go horizontally or vertically.

7	4	16	2	6
12	20	9	24	18
1	15	5	3	21
30	8	14	10	27

Q3 Work out the cost of the following.

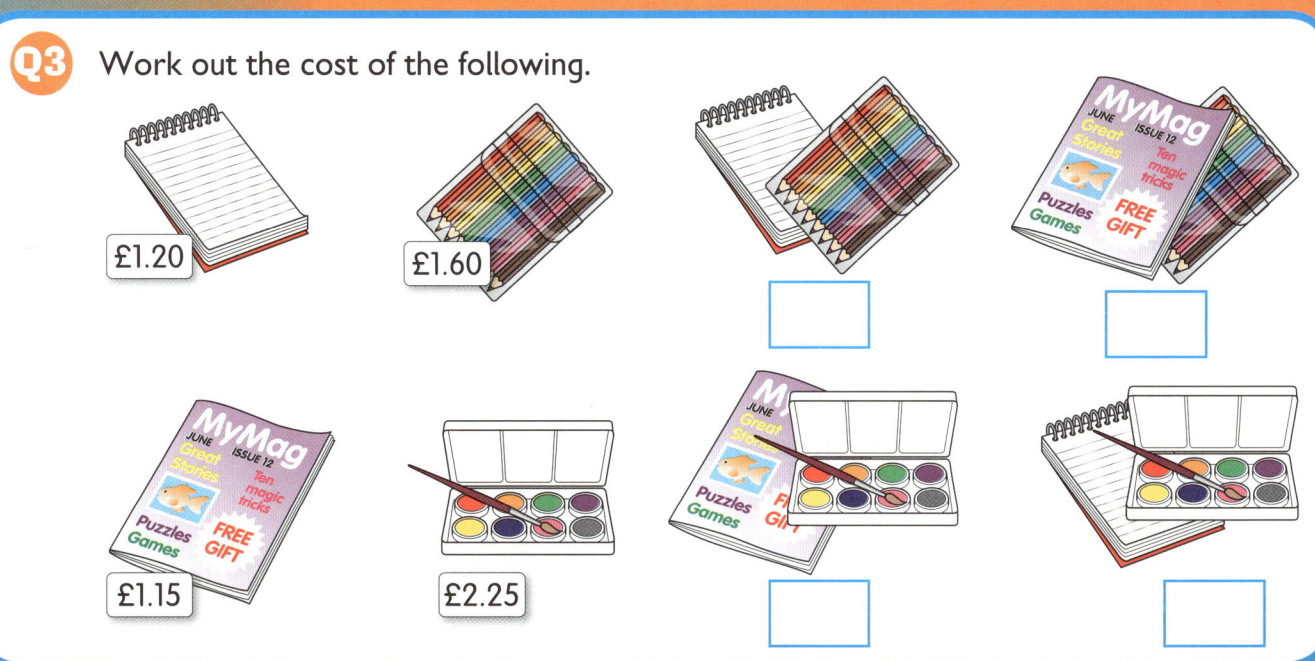

£1.20   £1.60

£1.15   £2.25

Look for examples of fractions and decimals in newspapers or magazines, around the home, or at the shops. Ask your child to explain to you what they mean.

Shape, space and measures 1

Q1 Complete the table.

Shape	Name of shape	Number of sides	Number of vertices	Number of lines of symmetry
1				
2				
3				
4				
5				
6				
7				

Q2 What time does each clock show?

   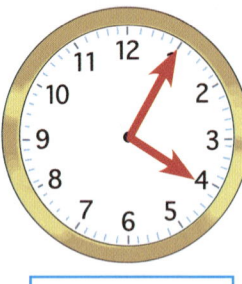

Draw hands on each clock to show the time.

2:25    5:55   10:40

Q3 Read each of these scales.

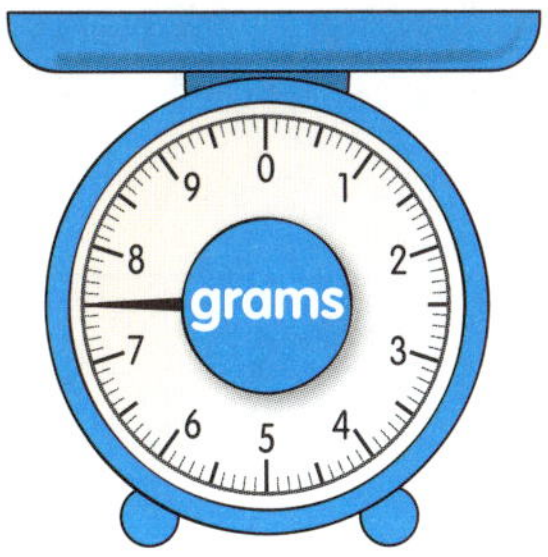

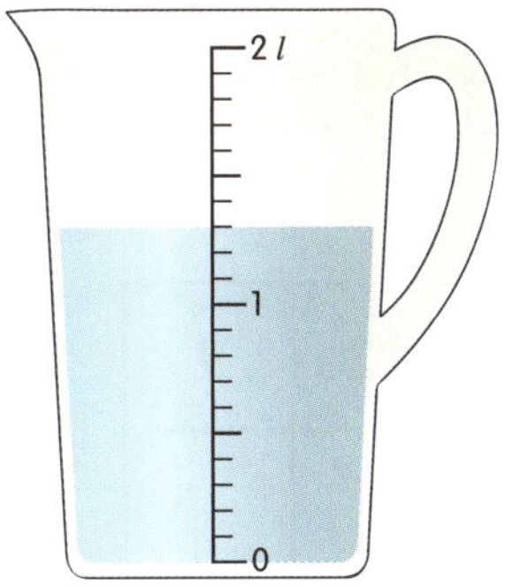

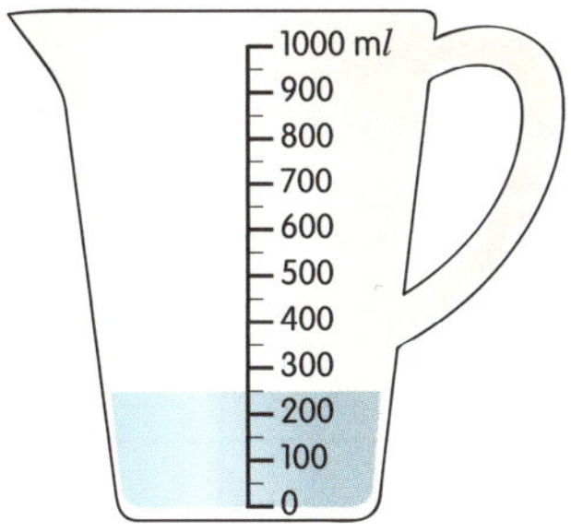

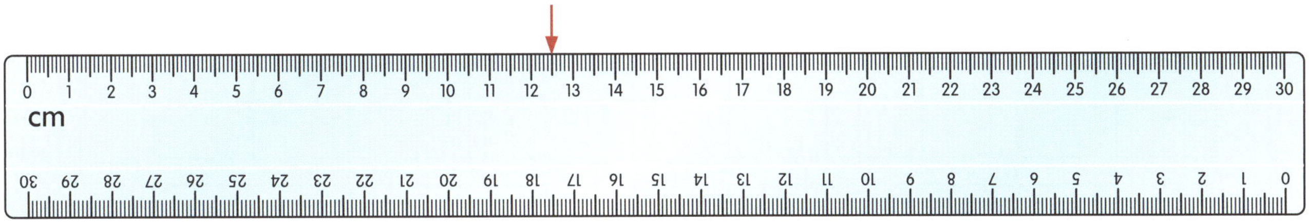

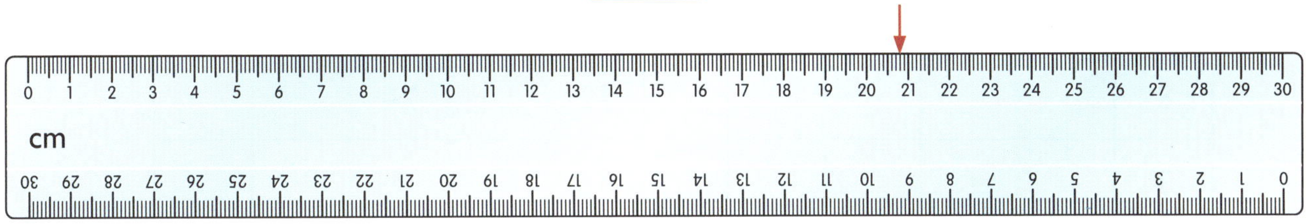

Q4 Draw lines of symmetry on these shapes.

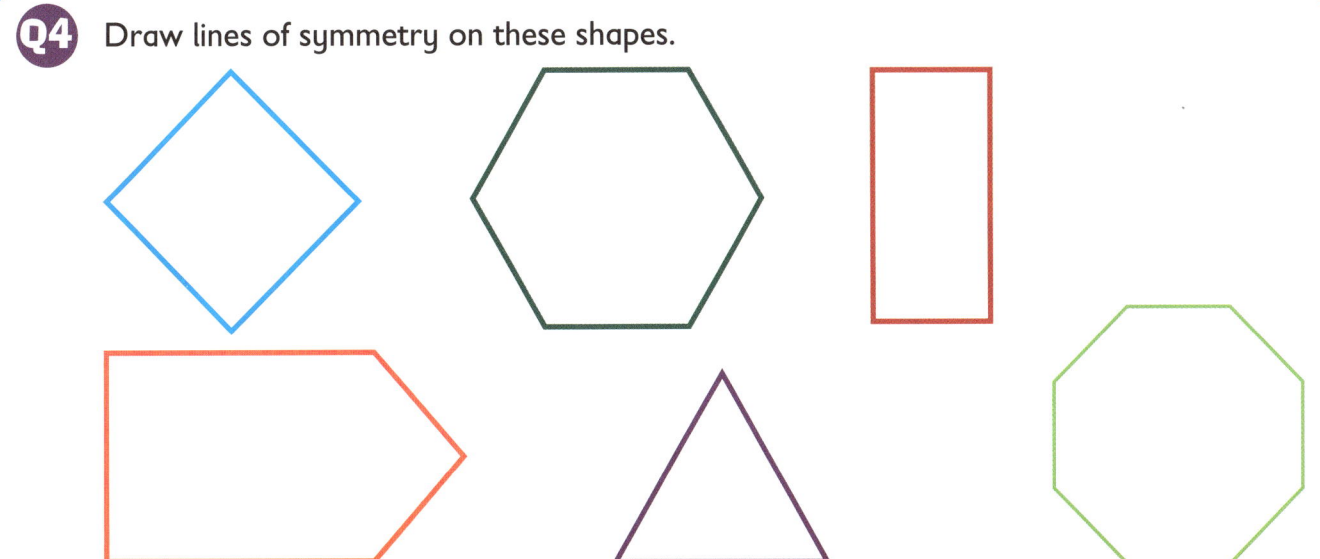

Your child needs to be able to name, and know the properties of, a range of 2-D and 3-D shapes. They also need to be able to estimate, compare and measure lengths, weights and capacities, and interpret the unnumbered divisions on a scale.

Problems and puzzles 1

Q1 Complete the tables.

+	8	5	12	9
6				
10			22	
7				
4				

−	3	6	4	7
14				
8		2		
17				
11				

×	4	8	7	9
6				
8				
3				
5				45

÷	2	3	6	9
18				
72		24		
36				
54				

Q2 How many different ways can you make 46, using any of the four operations and some or all of these numbers?

Q3 How many 1-, 2- and 3-digit numbers can you make using these digits?

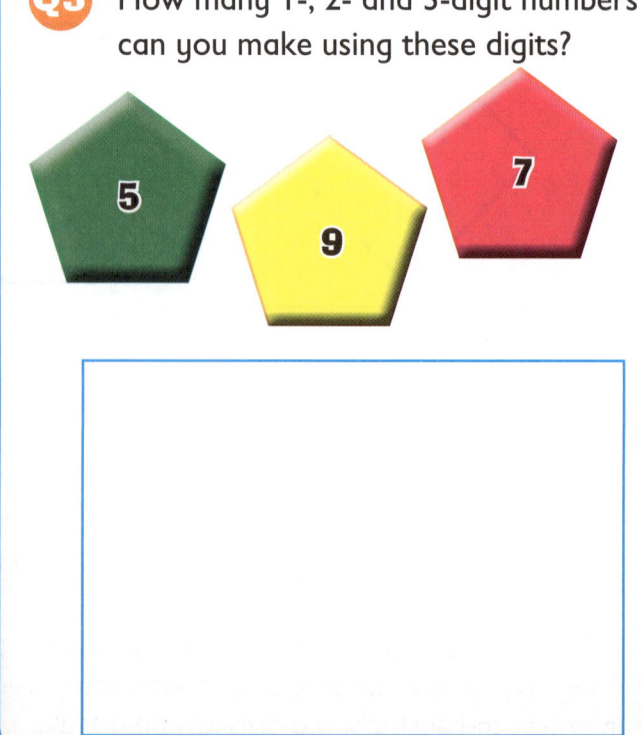

Q4 Answer these.

A bucket holds 40 litres of water. How many 5 litre jugs can you fill?

There are 48 chocolates in a box. One-third of the chocolates are dark chocolate and the rest are milk chocolate. How many milk chocolates are there in the box?

Louise has 5 metres of lace. She cuts it into 10 equal pieces. If Louise uses 3 pieces for her dress, how much lace is left?

Samson is 104 cm. His older brother is 17 cm taller. How tall is Samson's brother?

There are 72 people on a bus. 36 people are sitting upstairs, 28 people are sitting downstairs and the rest are standing. How many people are standing?

Thomas spends £1.32 at the shops. What change does he get back from £5?

Q5 Write the digits 3 to 9 on the grid so that each row and column of three digits totals the numbers in the stars.

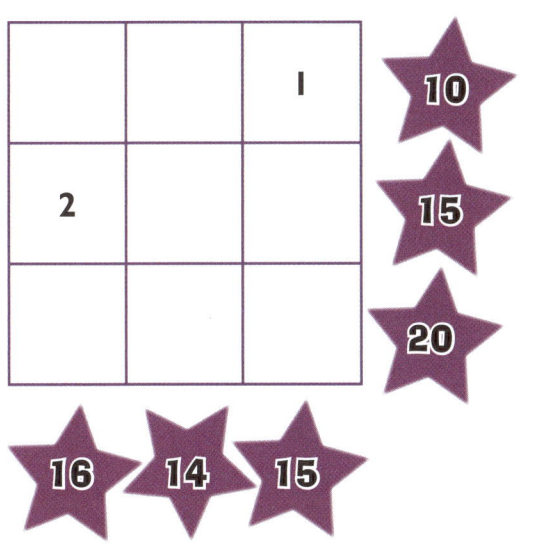

Q6 The number in each star is the difference between the two numbers in the circles either side of it. Write the missing numbers in the circles and stars.

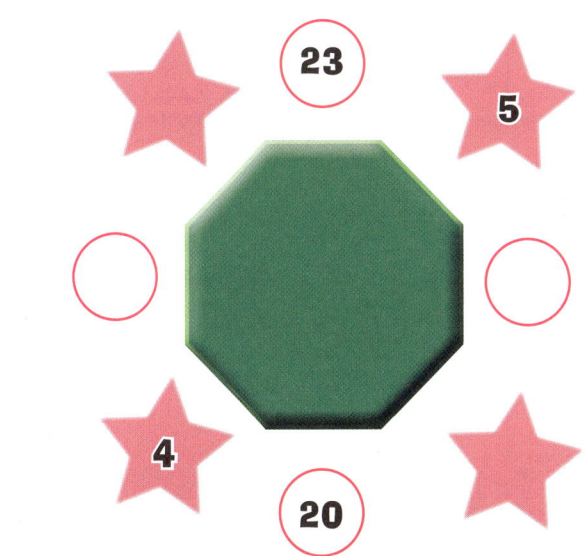

Your child needs to be able to use and apply their mathematical knowledge to solve problems and puzzles in the real world. Wherever possible, ask your child word problems similar to those in Q3.

Quick Check 1

Q1 Numbers

Continue the pattern.

650, 600, 550, ☐, ☐, ☐

Order the numbers, smallest first.

576, 327, 105, 567, 501, 322

☐ ☐ ☐ ☐ ☐ ☐

Fill in the missing numbers.

578 = ☐ + 70 + 8

432 = 400 + ☐ + 2

Q2 Addition and subtraction

Write the missing numbers.

9 + 8 = ☐   18 − 2 = ☐

7 + ☐ = 16   13 − 5 = ☐

☐ − 3 = 12   ☐ + 5 = 17

5 + 9 + 7 = ☐   11 − ☐ = 9

20 − 12 = ☐   3 + 8 + 6 = ☐

Q3 Multiplication and division

Write the missing numbers.

7 × 8 = ☐   42 ÷ 6 = ☐

48 ÷ 4 = ☐   9 × 4 = ☐

45 ÷ 5 = ☐   63 ÷ 9 = ☐

3 × ☐ = 24   7 × ☐ = 49

☐ ÷ 9 = 4   10 × ☐ = 500

Q4 Fractions and decimals

What fraction is coloured? ☐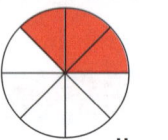

Order the fractions, smallest first.

$\frac{3}{10}, \frac{1}{2}, \frac{1}{4}, \frac{1}{10}, \frac{3}{4}$

☐ ☐ ☐ ☐ ☐

What is the 1 worth in each of these amounts?

£2.15 ☐   £7.41 ☐

Q5 Shape, space and measures

How many corners does a pentagon have? ☐

Draw all the lines of symmetry.

What's the weight?

Show 8.35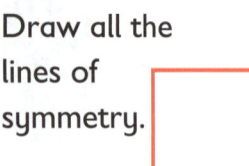

Q6 Problems and puzzles

Write, smallest to largest, all the different 1-, 2- and 3-digit numbers you can make using the digits 2, 4 and 8, e.g. 248. ☐

Simon gets on a train at 3:15. His journey last $1\frac{1}{2}$ hr. At what time does Simon get off the train? ☐

There are 52 playing cards in a pack. Paul shares them evenly between 4 people. How many cards does each person get? ☐

16

Time Test 1

Time how long it takes you to answer the following questions

Q1 8 + 7 + 4 = ☐

Q2 Order the numbers, smallest first.
546, 745, 576, 754, 364
☐ ☐ ☐ ☐ ☐

Q3 6 × 3 = ☐

Q4 What is the value of the 8 in 582?
☐

Q5 18 − 7 = ☐

Q6 Continue the pattern.
387, 391, 395, ☐, ☐, ☐

Q7 96 ÷ 8 = ☐

Q8 52 × 100 = ☐

Q9 What fraction is shaded?
☐
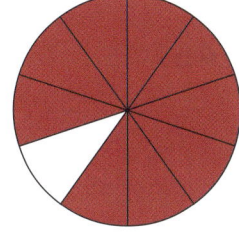

Q10 65 + 80 = ☐

Q11 What is the time?

☐

Q12 77 − 30 = ☐

Q13 6800 ÷ 100 = ☐

Q14 Circle the largest fraction.
$\frac{3}{4}$ $\frac{1}{10}$ $\frac{1}{2}$

Q15 Show 350 ml
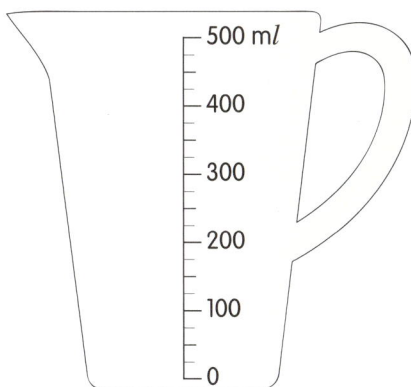

Q16 450 × 10 = ☐

Q17 £1.43 + £5.54 = ☐

Q18 How many lines of symmetry does a regular octagon have?
☐

Q19 279 = 200 + ☐ + 9

Q20 67 + 8 = ☐

Score	Time

Numbers 2

Q1 Put each set of numbers in order, smallest first.

| 684 | 846 | 648 | 468 | 864 | 486 |

| 538 | 385 | 853 | 583 | 835 | 358 |

| 5938 | 4736 | 2094 | 4728 | 8752 | 2328 |

Look at all the numbers in the blue boxes.
Write these number in order, smallest first.

Look at all the numbers in the red boxes.
Write these numbers in order, smallest first.

Q2 Round each of these numbers to the nearest 10.

586   221   467   744

Round each of these numbers to the nearest 10 and 100.

6372   1438   8585   3131

Game: Round to 10

You need: two 1 – 6 dice, counters

- Before you start, decide who will have which colour tower.
- Take turns to:
  – roll the dice and use the two numbers to make a two-digit number,

  e.g. could be either

  62 or 26
  – round the number to the nearest multiple of 10, i.e. 62 would be 60.
  – put a counter on that multiple on your tower.
- The winner is the first player to put a counter on each of their multiples of 10.

70 | 70
60 | 60
50 | 50
40 | 40
30 | 30
20 | 20
10 | 10

Q3 What is the value of the red digit in each of these numbers?

2038 ☐   8135 ☐

7461 ☐   1098 ☐

5473 ☐   3535 ☐

4837 ☐   6202 ☐

Q4 Complete each number sentence.

4625 = 4000 + ☐ + 20 + 5   1284 = ☐ + 200 + 80 + 4

3917 = 3000 + ☐ + ☐ + 7   5871 = 5000 + ☐ + ☐ + 1

8259 = ☐ + 200 + ☐ + 9   ☐ = 3000 + 800 + 70 + 2

Being able to round numbers to the nearest 10 and 100 will help your child with estimating answers to calculations involving three-digit numbers, e.g. 547 + 321 ≈ 550 + 320 = 870.

Addition and subtraction 2

You can use known addition and subtraction number facts to help work out the answers when adding or subtracting multiples of 10, 100 and 1000.

Example
7 + 5 = 12
So: 70 + 50 = 120
700 + 500 = 1200
7000 + 5000 = 12 000

Q1 Add together pairs of numbers next to each other and write the answer in the box above.

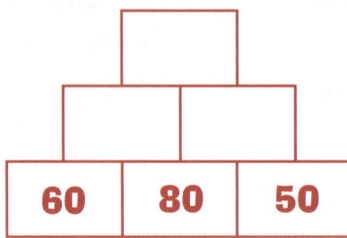 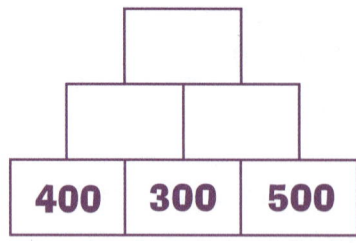 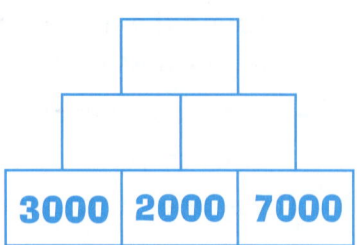

Find the difference between pairs of numbers next to each other and write the answer in the box above.

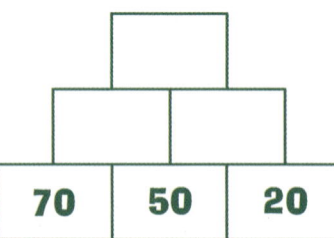 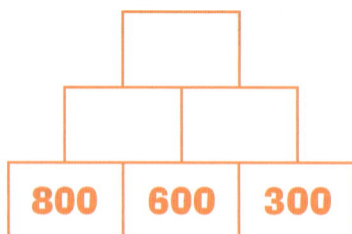 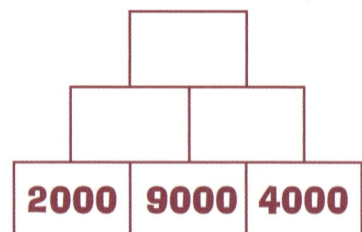

Q2 Add the two balls together.

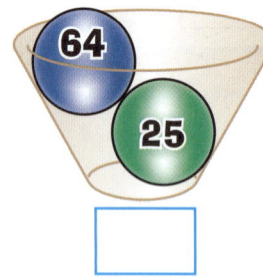 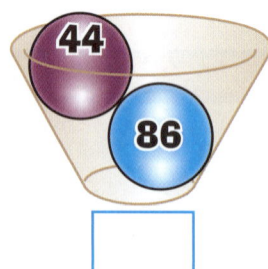 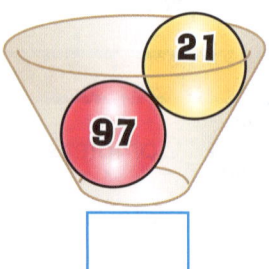

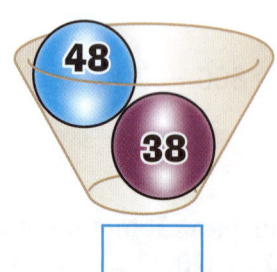 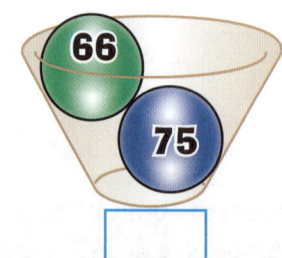 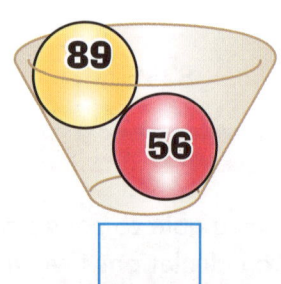

Game: Adding to or subtracting from the stars

You need: 1–6 dice, counters

- Take turns to:
  - say a number on a star
  - roll the dice
  - add or subtract the dice number to or from the star number
  - say the calculation and put a counter on that answer on the grid.
- If you can't find that answer on the grid, miss that turn.
- The winner is the first player to complete a line of 4 counters. A line can go horizontally or vertically.

Stars: 26, 53, 44, 75, 17, 68

54	47	72	74	30	43
11	81	48	23	64	20
19	69	41	79	51	13
25	73	28	63	46	58
66	18	49	56	74	71
32	38	80	12	49	21

Q3 Find the difference between the two balls.

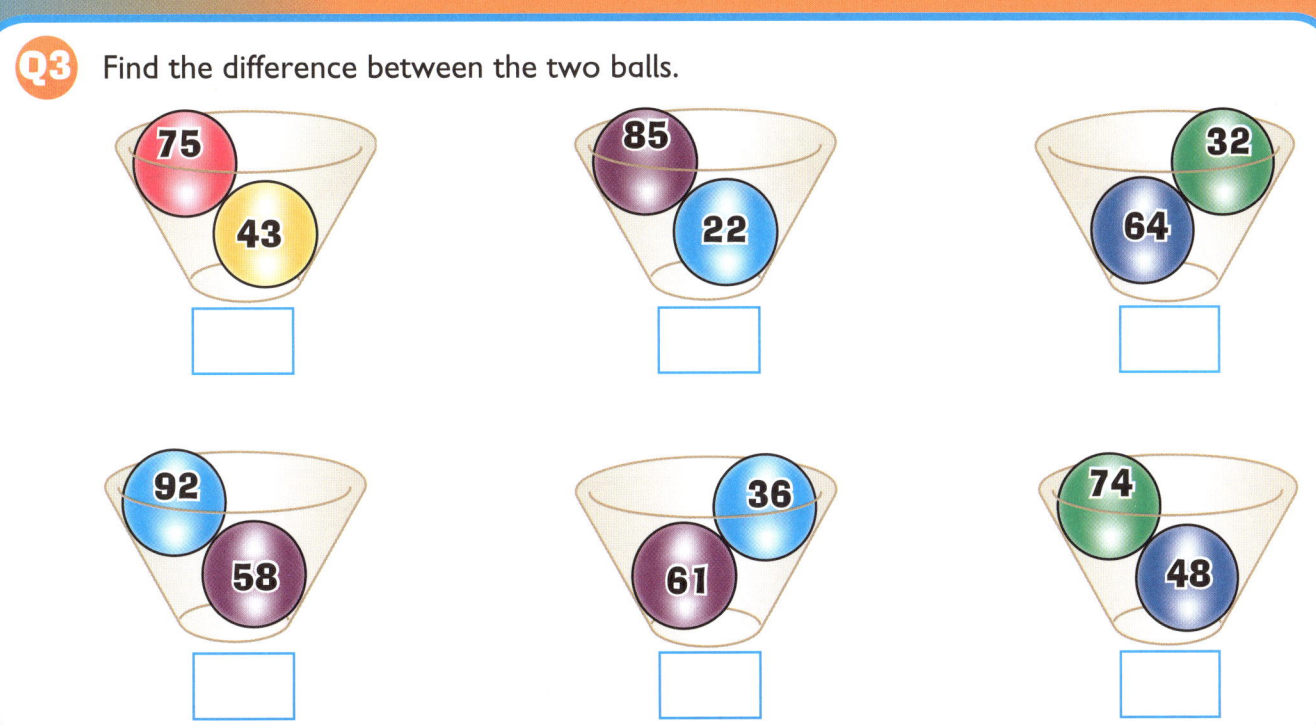

When adding and subtracting pairs of two-digit numbers such as 56 + 39 and 84 − 37, your child may not at first be able to do this entirely in their head. If so, encourage them to make jottings to help them remember what they are unable to hold in their head.

Multiplication and division 2

Q1 Answer these.

7 × 5 = ☐   4 × 8 = ☐   5 × 4 = ☐

56 ÷ 8 = ☐   45 ÷ 5 = ☐   28 ÷ 7 = ☐

40 ÷ 10 = ☐   6 × 12 = ☐   7 × 3 = ☐

6 × 6 = ☐   48 ÷ 4 = ☐   132 ÷ 11 = ☐

8 × 11 = ☐   12 × 10 = ☐   6 × 7 = ☐

54 ÷ 9 = ☐   54 ÷ 6 = ☐   96 ÷ 12 = ☐

2 × 7 = ☐   8 × 9 = ☐   49 ÷ 7 = ☐

You can use known multiplication and division number facts to help work out the answers when multiplying and dividing multiples of 10 and 100.

Example
4 × 7 = 28
So: 40 × 7 = 280
    4 × 700 = 2800

Example
72 ÷ 6 = 12
So: 720 ÷ 6 = 120
    720 ÷ 60 = 12

Q2 Answer these.

30 × 9 = ☐   80 × 50 = ☐   70 × 11 = ☐

560 ÷ 8 = ☐   420 ÷ 6 = ☐   640 ÷ 80 = ☐

6 × 40 = ☐   60 × 8 = ☐   800 ÷ 10 = ☐

250 ÷ 5 = ☐   320 ÷ 40 = ☐   8 × 120 = ☐

400 × 8 = ☐   30 × 70 = ☐   50 × 100 = ☐

350 ÷ 70 = ☐   630 ÷ 9 = ☐   1080 ÷ 90 = ☐

3 × 600 = ☐   490 ÷ 7 = ☐   200 × 60 = ☐

Game: The Multiples Game

You need: pencil, paperclip, 20 counters: 10 of one colour, 10 of another colour

- Before you start choose who will have which colour counters.
- Take turns to place one of your counters on a number on the grid, making sure not to cover up the number.
- Keep going until you have each placed all your 10 counters on the grid.

Rule: Only one counter can go on each number.

- Now take turns to:
  – spin the spinner
  – take a counter off the grid showing a multiple of that number, but only if the counter is in your colour.
- The winner is the first player to collect all their counters.

66	45	10	28	33	63
6	8	36	20	48	15
35	12	32	22	18	56
40	54	60	14	72	88
24	27	42	30	21	16

Q3 Double each of these numbers. Halve each of these numbers.

54   76   60   89   300   80   94   78   700   56

Using knowledge of their times tables facts as well as being able to multiply multiples of 10 and 100, will help your child when multiplying larger numbers such as 62 × 8 and 268 × 7.

Fractions and decimals 2

Q1 What is the value of the red digit in each of these decimals?

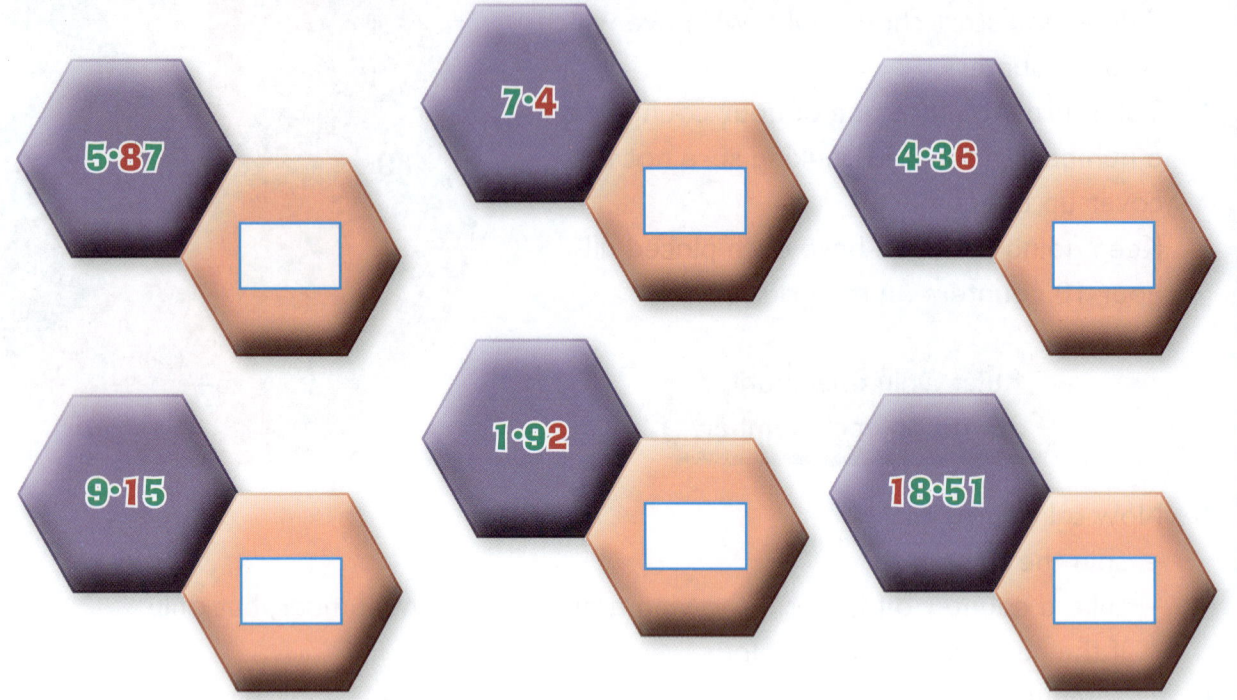

Complete each number sentence.

2·46 = 2 + ☐ + 0·06

27·93 = 20 + 7 + ☐ + ☐

☐ = 7 + 0·9 + 0·01

8·35 = 8 + 0·3 + ☐

4·12 = 4 + ☐ + ☐

☐ = 9 + 0·5 + 0·06

Q2 Complete the fractions.

$\dfrac{1}{3} = \dfrac{4}{☐}$ $\dfrac{1}{2} = \dfrac{☐}{8}$ $\dfrac{3}{☐} = \dfrac{9}{12}$ $\dfrac{☐}{5} = \dfrac{3}{15}$

$\dfrac{2}{3} = \dfrac{4}{☐}$ $\dfrac{1}{4} = \dfrac{☐}{20}$ $\dfrac{2}{☐} = \dfrac{8}{12}$ $\dfrac{☐}{10} = \dfrac{9}{30}$

$\dfrac{2}{5} = \dfrac{4}{☐}$ $\dfrac{7}{10} = \dfrac{☐}{50}$ $\dfrac{3}{☐} = \dfrac{9}{15}$ $\dfrac{☐}{5} = \dfrac{12}{15}$

Game: Finding tenths

You need: two 1–6 dice, counters

- Take turns to:
  - roll both dice, e.g. 2 and 5 (if you roll a double, roll the dice again)
  - place one of your counters on the grid on a decimal which is between the two dice numbers, e.g. 4·7.
- The winner is the first player to complete a line of 4 counters. A line can go horizontally or vertically.

2·6	6·2	4·8	5·4	1·2	3·9
6·4	4·1	3·3	1·6	2·9	5·5
4·7	2·5	1·1	3·2	5·8	6·7
1·7	5·1	6·9	2·1	3·6	4·4
3·4	1·8	5·8	6·6	4·2	2·3
5·6	3·1	2·7	4·3	6·5	1·4

Q3 Change these fractions to decimals.

$\frac{1}{2} = \square$ $\frac{1}{10} = \square$ $\frac{1}{4} = \square$ $\frac{6}{10} = \square$

$\frac{3}{4} = \square$ $\frac{3}{10} = \square$ $\frac{8}{10} = \square$ $\frac{4}{10} = \square$

$2\frac{2}{10} = \square$ $3\frac{7}{10} = \square$ $1\frac{9}{10} = \square$ $5\frac{3}{4} = \square$

Your child needs to be able to recognise equivalent fractions as well as recognise and write decimal equivalents for ¼, ½, ¾ and tenths. They also need to have a secure understanding of place value for decimal numbers up to two decimal places like the red numbers in **Q1**.

Shape, space and measures 2

Q1 Complete the table.

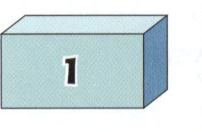      

Solid	Name of solid	Number of faces	Number of vertices	Number of edges
1				
2				
3				
4				
5				
6				
7				

Q2 What time does each clock show?

Draw hands on each clock to show the time.

5:38 1:54 11:06

Q3 Answer these.

1·2 m = [ ] cm   6 kg = [ ] g

$\frac{1}{2}$ l = [ ] ml   40 mm = [ ] cm

2500 g = [ ] kg   7 l = [ ] ml

1 hour = [ ] min   80 cm = [ ] mm

$\frac{3}{4}$ kg = [ ] g   3500 ml = [ ] l

$\frac{1}{4}$ km = [ ] m   1 year = [ ] months

$\frac{3}{10}$ l = [ ] ml $\frac{7}{10}$ kg = [ ] g

Q4 Calculate the perimeter and area of these shapes.

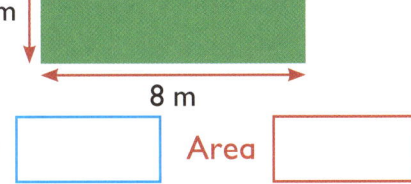

Perimeter [ ]   Area [ ]

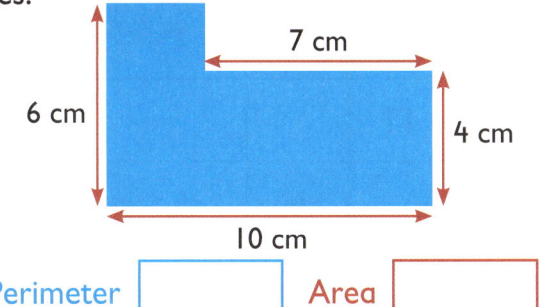

Perimeter [ ]   Area [ ]

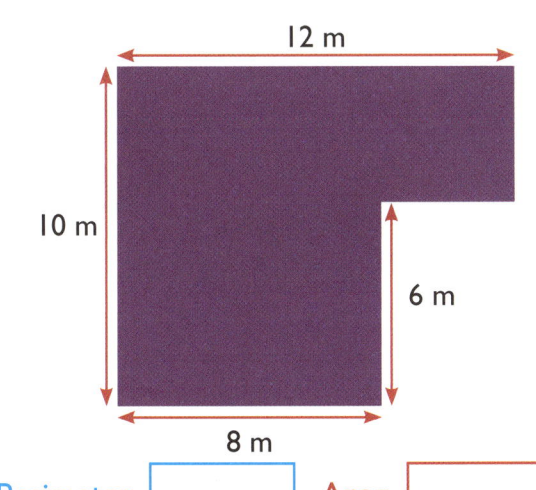

Perimeter [ ]   Area [ ]

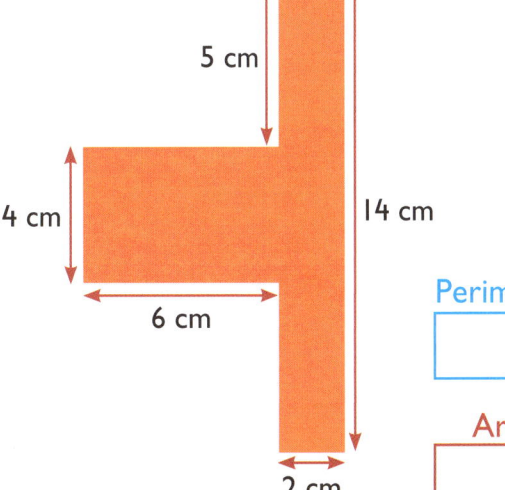

Perimeter [ ]   Area [ ]

Your child needs to be able to use standard units for length, mass, capacity and time and be able to convert between different units of measure. They should also be able to work out the perimeter and area of simple rectilinear shapes.

Problems and puzzles 2

Q1 Complete the grids.

◇	○	◇+○	◇−○
12	8		
17	11		
25			12
	25		11

◇	○	◇+○	◇×○
6	3		
8			56
4		13	
		12	60

◇	○	◇−○	◇×○
9			18
	8	2	
11			121
		4	4

◇	○	◇+○	◇÷○
32			4
	4		3
48		54	
	5	50	

Q2 How many different ways can you make $5\frac{1}{2}$? Here is one example.

$$8 - 2\frac{1}{2} = 5\frac{1}{2}$$

Q3 How many different ways can you make 25 using any of the four operations and some or all of these numbers?

28

Q4 Answer these.

Fiona starts her homework at 4:05 pm and finishes at 5:25 pm. How long does Fiona spend on her homework?

There were 84 people at a party. Of these $\frac{3}{4}$ were adults and the rest were children. How many children were at the party?

Henry the chef is preparing for a party and needs to use 100 eggs. How many boxes of 12 eggs does he need to buy?

A supermarket has specials on yoghurt and orange juice. Buy 2 orange juice for £3 and 4 yoghurts for £1.50. Leroy buys 4 orange juice and 8 yoghurts. How much change does he get back from £20?

On Friday, Lee drove 120 km from his home to his parents' home. On Saturday he drove a further 45 km to visit his aunt. On Sunday he drove back home from his aunt's home via his parents' home. Altogether how many kilometres did he drive at the weekend?

Q5 Using each of the digits 1 to 9 only once, complete these four times tables facts.

☐ × ☐ = 56

☐ × ☐ = 24

☐ × ☐ = 27

☐☐ × ☐ = 60

Q6 Write each of the digits 1 to 5 once only in each row and column. Use the < and > signs to help you.

☐ ☐ > ☐ ☐ > ☐

☐ > ☐ ☐ 4 ☐

☐ ☐ 3 ☐ ☐

☐ < ☐ ☐ ☐ ☐
      ∧   ∧

3 ☐ ☐ > ☐ ☐

Find times at home, when out shopping or visiting other places to ask your child a word problem like those in Q3. Try not to just focus on the answer to the problem, but talk to your child about the way they work things out.

Quick Check 2

Q1 Numbers

Round these numbers to the nearest 10.

684 ☐   137 ☐   435 ☐

Order the numbers, smallest first.
6857, 5768, 6875, 5678, 3498

☐ ☐ ☐ ☐ ☐

Fill in the missing numbers.

4529 = ☐ + 500 + 20 + 9

7218 = 7000 + ☐ + 10 + 8

Q2 Addition and subtraction

Write the missing numbers.

70 + 80 = ☐   31 − 7 = ☐

67 + 5 = ☐   63 − 22 = ☐

58 + 65 = ☐   900 − 400 = ☐

97 − 53 = ☐   45 + ☐ = 92

81 − ☐ = 39   36 + 28 = ☐

Q3 Multiplication and division

Write the missing numbers.

12 × 9 = ☐   600 ÷ 10 = ☐

42 ÷ 6 = ☐   80 × 40 = ☐

28 ÷ 4 = ☐   270 ÷ 30 = ☐

8 × ☐ = 64   6 × ☐ = 180

☐ ÷ 9 = 4   ☐ × 30 = 1200

Q4 Fractions and decimals

Fill in the missing numbers.

6·72 = 6 + ☐ + 0·02

13·53 = 10 + 3 + 0·5 + ☐

Complete the fractions

$\frac{1}{3} = \frac{5}{☐}$ $\frac{2}{3} = \frac{☐}{6}$ $\frac{☐}{10} = \frac{4}{40}$

Write each of these as a fraction.

0·4 ☐    0·75 ☐

Q5 Shape, space and measures

How many verticies does a cuboid have? ☐

90 cm = ☐ mm

$\frac{1}{4}$ l = ☐ ml

300 g = ☐ kg

1 week = ☐ days

What is the perimeter of this shape? ☐

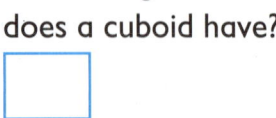

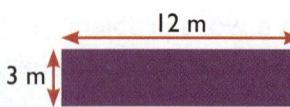

Show 4.27

Q6 Problems and puzzles

Use the digits 2 to 9 only once to complete these calculations.

☐ + ☐ = 13

☐ − ☐ = 5

☐ × ☐ = 24

☐ ÷ ☐ = 3

Share £12 and £6 equally among 3 children. How much does each child get? ☐

Time Test 2

Time how long it takes you to answer the following questions

Q1 What is the value of the 7 in 6179? ☐

Q2 60 + 50 = ☐

Q3 Order the numbers, smallest first.
3847, 5462, 3756, 3865, 5261
☐ ☐ ☐ ☐ ☐

Q4 90 × 70 = ☐

Q5 9000 − 3000 = ☐

Q6 Continue the pattern.
4·5, 5, 5·5, 6, ☐ , ☐ , ☐

Q7 72 ÷ 12 = ☐

Q8 82 − 35 = ☐

Q9 What is $\frac{9}{10}$ as a decimal? ☐

Q10 What is the time?

☐

Q11 57·32 = 50 + 7 + 0·3 + ☐

Q12 150 ÷ 30 = ☐

Q13 $\frac{\square}{5} = \frac{8}{20}$

Q14 What is the value of the 5 in 4·53? ☐

Q15 5500 ml = ☐ l

Q16 68 + 55 = ☐

Q17 £4.87 − £1.36 = ☐

Q18 What is the area of this shape? ☐

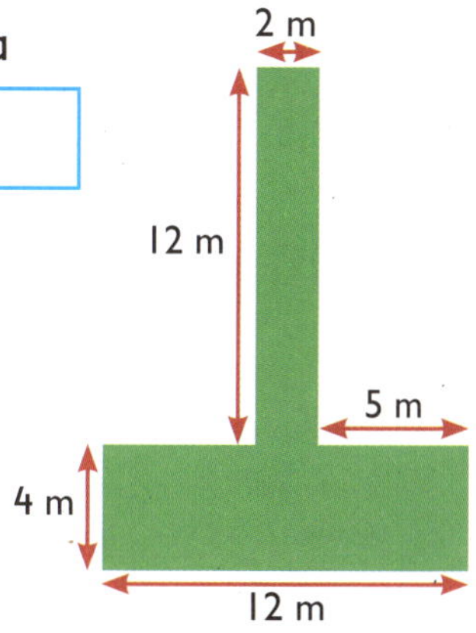

(shape with dimensions: 2 m, 12 m, 5 m, 4 m, 12 m)

Q19 What is the perimeter of the shape above? ☐

Q20 Round 5362 to the nearest:
10 ☐   100 ☐

Score	Time

Answers

Numbers 1
Page 4
1. 435, 438, 441, 444, 447, 450, 453, 456, 459, 462
706, 711, 716, 721, 726, 731, 736, 741, 746, 751
716, 712, 708, 704, 700, 696, 692, 688, 684, 680
300, 350, 400, 450, 500, 550, 600, 650, 700, 750

2.
695	<	703		544	>	424		756	>	675
119	<	209		843	>	834		297	<	379
209		379		424		675		703		834
119		297		544		695		756		843

Page 5
3. 697 = 600 + 90 + 7   423 = 400 + 20 + 3
391 = 300 + 90 + 1   725 = 700 + 20 + 5
284 = 200 + 80 + 4   139 = 100 + 30 + 9 *
572 = 500 + 70 + 2 *   918 = 900 + 10 + 8 *
* Other answers are possible

Addition and subtraction 1
Page 6
1. 9 + 4 = 13   6 + 11 = 17   17 − 8 = 9
7 + 7 = 14   13 − 6 = 7   14 + 6 = 20
15 − 8 = 7   13 + 5 = 18   16 − 3 = 13
18 − 12 = 6   19 − 10 = 9   12 + 7 = 19
8 − 5 = 3   7 + 4 + 5 = 16 17 − 4 = 13
6 + 14 = 20   12 + 7 = 19   3 + 8 + 6 = 17
20 − 12 = 8   14 − 9 = 5   15 + 3 = 18
6 + 8 + 9 = 23 8 + 8 = 16   16 − 14 = 2

2. 43 113   26 76
    35 105   11 121
     7 127   24 124

Page 7
3.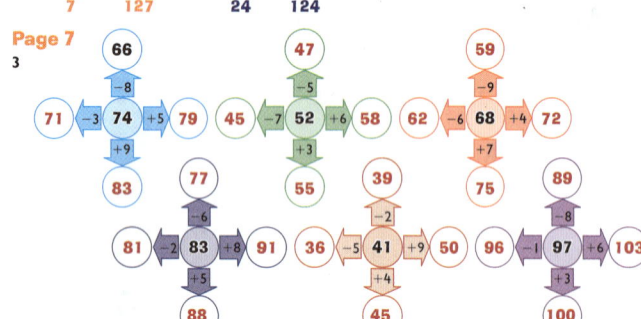

Multiplication and division 1
Page 8
1.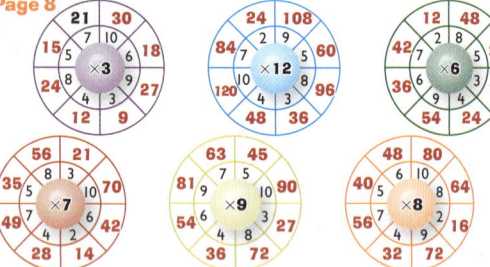

2. ÷6 42 7 36 6 54 9 30 5 12 2 60 10 24 4 48 8 18 3
   ÷8 24 3 80 10 48 6 16 2 72 9 64 8   40 5 56 7 32 4
   ÷4 20 5 8 2 36 9 28 7 40 10 16 4   24 6 32 8 12 3
   ÷9 36 4 18 2 81 9 45 5 63 7 90 10 27 3 72 8 54 6
   ÷3 12 4 27 9 18 6 24 8 6 2 15 5   21 7 9 3 30 10
   ÷7 63 9 70 10 14 2 28 4 56 8 49 7   35 5 42 6 21 3

Page 9
3. 670 67 6700   30 300   3
   520 52 5200   870 8700 87
   830 83 8300   520 5200 52
   240 24 2400   600 6000 60
   750 75 7500   180 1800 18
   380 38 3800   290 2900 29
   910 91 9100   40 400   4

Fractions and decimals 1
Page 10
1. $\frac{1}{4}, \frac{2}{3}, \frac{3}{4}, \frac{5}{6}$ $\frac{1}{8}, \frac{1}{5}, \frac{3}{5}, \frac{3}{10}$

2.
$\frac{1}{2}$	>	$\frac{1}{3}$		$\frac{1}{6}$	<	$\frac{1}{4}$		$\frac{1}{5}$	>	$\frac{1}{8}$
$\frac{1}{10}$	<	$\frac{1}{6}$		$\frac{1}{9}$	<	$\frac{1}{7}$		$\frac{1}{3}$	>	$\frac{1}{5}$
$\frac{1}{8}$		$\frac{1}{7}$		$\frac{1}{6}$		$\frac{1}{5}$		$\frac{1}{4}$		$\frac{1}{3}$
$\frac{1}{10}$		$\frac{1}{9}$		$\frac{1}{6}$		$\frac{1}{5}$		$\frac{1}{3}$		$\frac{1}{2}$

Page 11
3. £2.80   £2.75   £3.40   £3.45

Shape, space and measures 1
Page 12
1.
	Shape	Name of shape	Number of sides	Number of vertices	Number of lines of symmetry
1		square	4	4	4
2		circle	1	0	infinity
3		hexagon	6	6	6
4		rectangle	4	4	2
5		triangle	3	3	3
6		pentagon	5	5	5
7		octagon	8	8	8

2. 7:10   11:20   4:05

Page 13
3. 2·4 kg (or 2 kg 400 g)   750 g (or $\frac{3}{4}$ kg)   1·3 l (or 1 l 300 ml)   250 ml (or $\frac{1}{4}$ l)
12·5 cm (or 125 mm)   20·8 cm (or 208 mm)

4.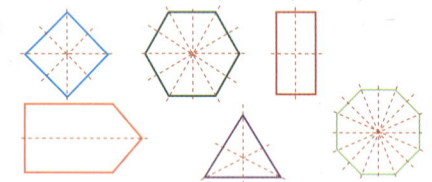

Problems and puzzles 1
Page 14
1.
+	8	5	12	9
6	14	11	18	15
10	18	15	22	19
7	15	12	19	16
4	12	9	16	13

−	3	6	4	7
14	11	8	10	7
8	5	2	4	1
17	14	11	13	10
11	8	5	7	4

×	4	8	7	9
6	24	48	42	54
8	32	64	56	72
3	12	24	21	27
5	20	40	35	45

÷	2	3	6	9
18	9	6	3	2
72	36	24	12	8
36	18	12	6	4
54	27	18	9	6

2. (6 × 8) − 2
(12 × 4) − 2
(3 × 12) + 6 + 4
(12 + 8 + 3) × 2
(3 × 8) + 12 + 4 + 6

3. 5, 7, 9
57, 59, 75, 79, 95, 97
579, 597, 759, 795, 957, 975
Other answers are possible.

Page 15
4. 8 jugs   32 milk chocolates   3·5 m (or 350 cm) left   121 cm tall   8 people   £3·68

5, 6.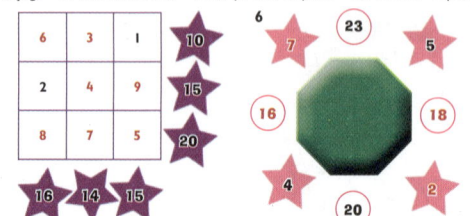

Other answers are possible.   Other answers are possible.

Quick Check 1
Page 16
1. **Numbers**
650, 600, 550, 500, 450, 400, 350
105, 322, 327, 501, 567, 576
578 = 500 + 70 + 8
432 = 400 + 30 + 2

2. **Addition and subtraction**
9 + 8 = 17   18 − 2 = 16
7 + 9 = 16   13 − 5 = 8
15 − 3 = 12   12 + 5 = 17
5 + 9 + 7 = 21 11 − 2 = 9
20 − 12 = 8   3 + 8 + 6 = 17

32